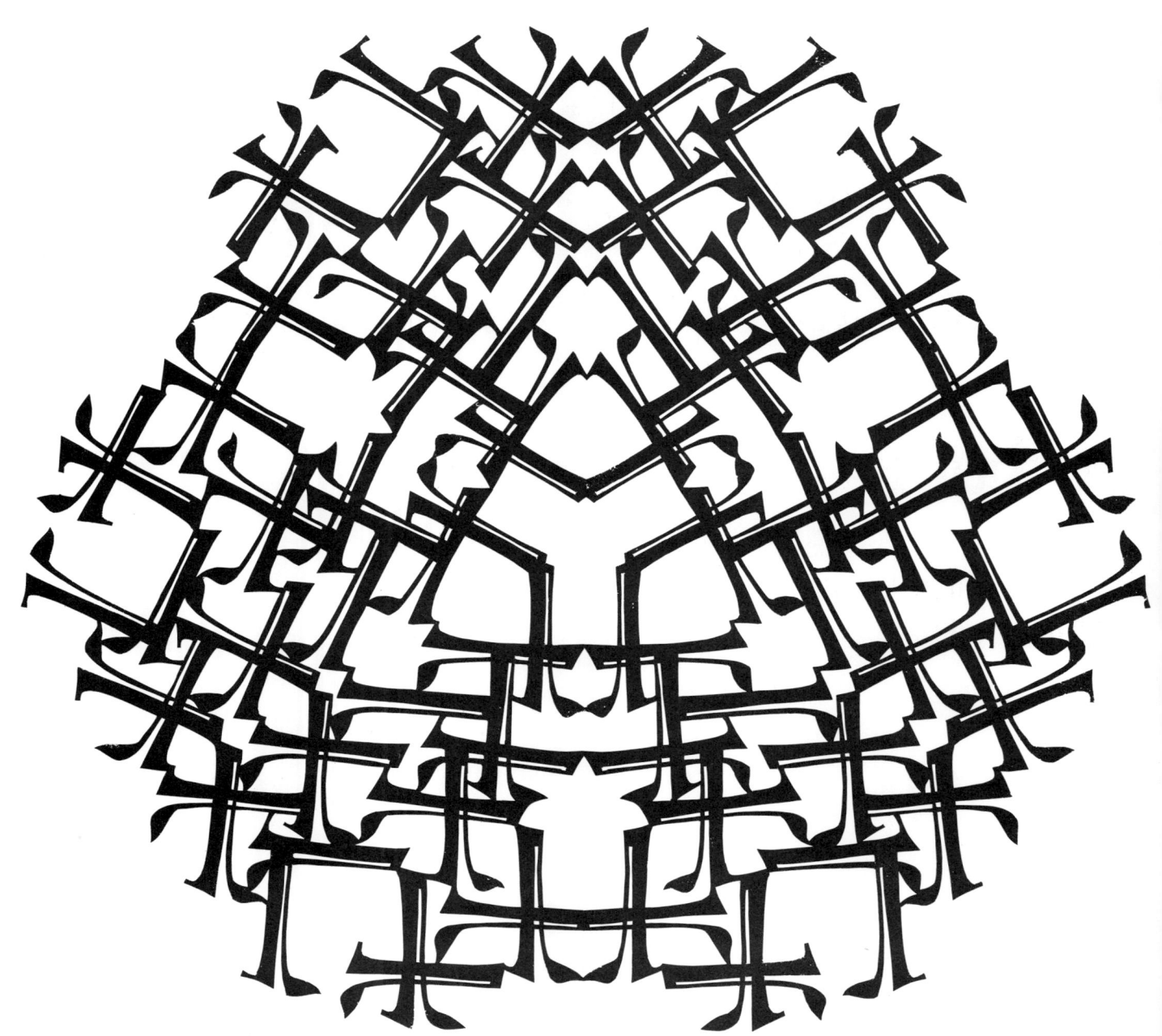

Calligraphic Cut-Paper Designs
FOR ARTISTS AND CRAFTSMEN

Arthur Baker

With an Introduction by
William Hogarth

Dover Publications, Inc.
New York

Introduction copyright © 1983 by William Hogarth.
All other contents copyright © 1983 by Arthur Baker.

Published in Canada by General Publishing Company, Ltd., 30 Lesmill Road, Don Mills, Toronto, Ontario.
Published in the United Kingdom by Constable and Company, Ltd., 10 Orange Street, London WC2H 7EG.

Calligraphic Cut-Paper Designs for Artists and Craftsmen is a new work, first published by Dover Publications, Inc., in 1983.

DOVER *Pictorial Archive* SERIES

Calligraphic Cut-Paper Designs for Artists and Craftsmen belongs to the Dover Pictorial Archive Series. Up to ten items may be reproduced in any single publication without payment to or permission from the publisher. Wherever possible include a credit line, indicating title, author and publisher. Please address the Publisher for permission to make more extensive use of illustrations in this volume than that authorized above. The reproduction of the entire book is prohibited.

Manufactured in the United States of America
Dover Publications, Inc.
180 Varick Street
New York, N.Y. 10014

Library of Congress Cataloging in Publication Data

Baker, Arthur.
   Calligraphic cut-paper designs for artists and craftsmen.

   (Dover pictorial archive series)
   1. Baker, Arthur. 2. Calligraphy. 3. Decoration and ornament. 4. Decoupage.
I. Title.
NK3631.B34A4   1982   745.6'1   82-9767
ISBN 0-486-20306-9 (pbk.)   AACR2

Identified Flying Objects
by William Hogarth

There is a tradition that paper was invented in China in 105 A.D. by one Ts'ai Lun, an official at the court of the emperor Ho Ti. Less apocryphal is the knowledge that Roman capital letters were perfected at almost exactly the same time, as evidenced in the surviving monuments in the Roman Forum and elsewhere in the classical Mediterranean world. In this book, these twin epiphanies coalesce in the delightful departure we have come to expect from the resourceful scribe Arthur Baker: the knife joins pen and brush in the transfiguration of plain paper.

Baker's researches have disclosed the method of construction of the Roman capitals—a system of pen manipulation that gave structure and beauty to the letters before they were V-cut in stone by masons. The results of his historical studies and artistic innovations have been amply shown in Baker's previous books for Dover: marvelous alphabets, letter forms and adventures in abstract calligraphy. These books have put Arthur Baker in the unique category of the most published calligrapher in the world today, certainly the most influential. Largely through his efforts, America has taken the lead in the field, and the New American Calligraphy is a recognized movement.

Paper folding and cutting have had a long history as folk art and craft around the world ever since Ts'ai Lun gave us one of the best and cheapest materials with which to create: delicate paper embroidery, kites and stencils; origami in Japan, shadow puppets in Indonesia and intricate silhouettes in Germany, Switzerland and Poland; lacy holiday designs that inspired the die-cut and embossed valentines and Christmas cards produced commercially in the nineteenth century. It is probably universal for children to discover that folded paper can be cut and unfolded to reveal a string of little paper people, introducing the world of *trompe-l'oeil*.

Fooling the eye is very much a part of the present collection of cut-paper designs by Arthur Baker. Whether the original stiff white paper is folded in thirds or quarters, in half again to sixths and eighths, or, with more difficulty, in fifths, the point of departure is simply a letter of the alphabet. Most of the underlying forms are derived from the Roman capitals or minuscules. The cut-outs were glued to black backgrounds. In the printed book, the majority of the designs appear in reverse (black on white), heightening the visual impact of the pen strokes that guided the hand of the paper cutter. For variety, about one fifth of the designs are shown in their original configuration of white on black.

What keeps the resulting forms from being static is the marvelous, manipulated calligraphy of the letter forms, which, in ensemble, suggest tondos, mandalas, cabalistic diagrams, outer-space novas, planets, flying objects. It isn't even necessary to *know* that each composition is letter-based, but the knowledge adds to the sense of appreciation for their accomplishment. The craftsperson who would attempt to create similar forms is urged to study the sophisticated calligraphy that is the basis of their success.

Of course it is quite simple to use the patterns as they are. As a part of the Dover Pictorial Archive series, the designs are highly reproducible and are meant to be used. But we also hope that you will be moved to create your own, thereby developing a sensitivity akin to Baker's and learning to move your pen (and blade) to create letters with organic integrity. Should you try your own cutting, your handiwork can be displayed against the sky, over patterned papers, sandwiched between plastic sheeting or glass, or used as stencils individually or one over the other.

And if you are inspired by these compositions, I think I can tell you why. In his exploration of the formal qualities of the twenty-six symbols that are the fundamental tools of learning and the vehicles of all knowledge, Arthur Baker has penetrated the mystery of creativity.

His ethereal choreography in two dimensions embodies a Jungian mystique of symbols, a wish that UFOs exist, a niggling wisp of suspicion that there may be a key to unlock infinity, a way to stuff the world's ills back and slam the lid on Pandora's box, even in this pragmatic age. The contemplation of these complex devices can be soothing, inspiring and bedeviling by turns. Beauty, and our response to it, is a necessity for health. Snowflakes melt. Paper lasts. Enjoy.

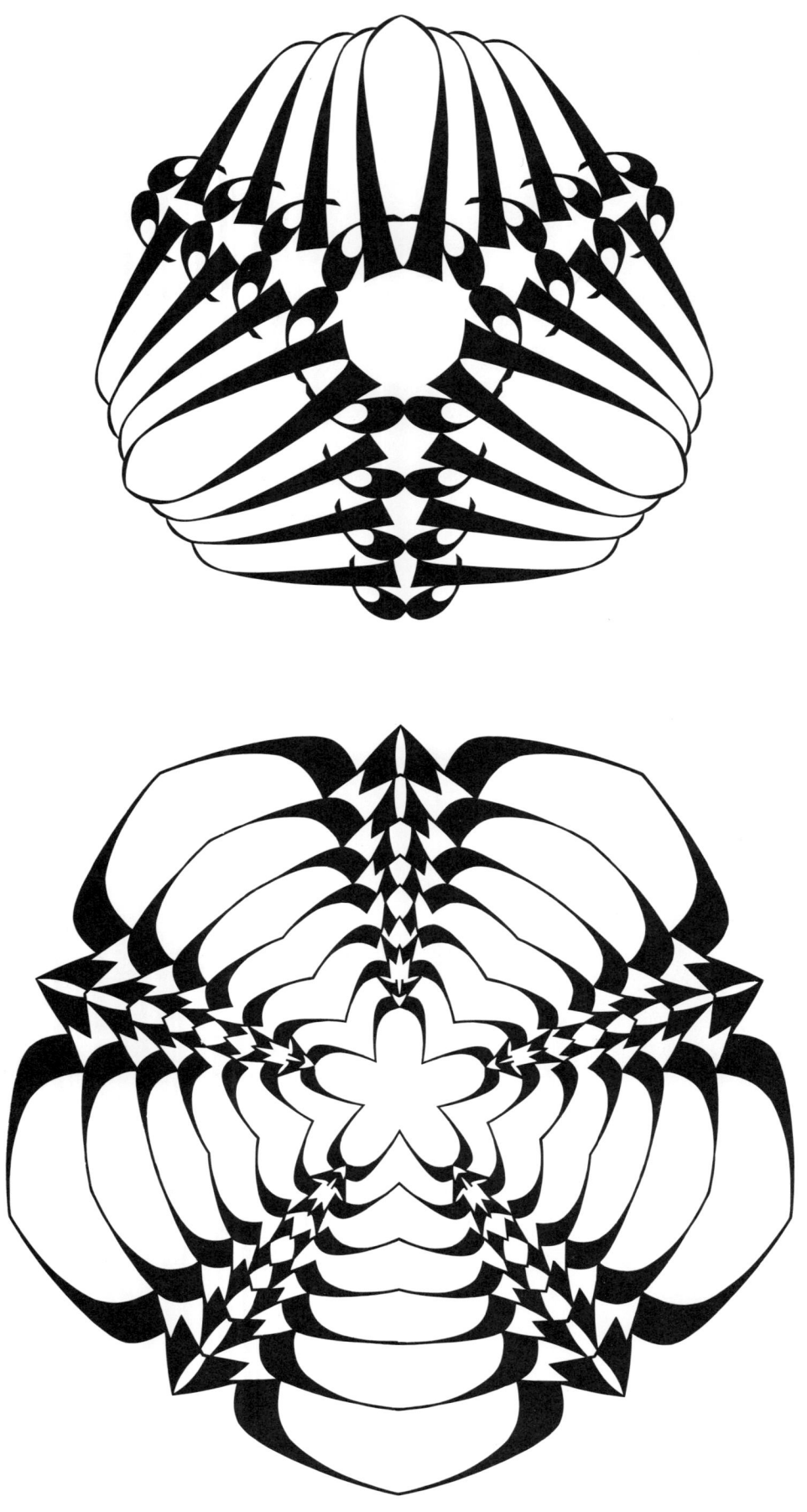

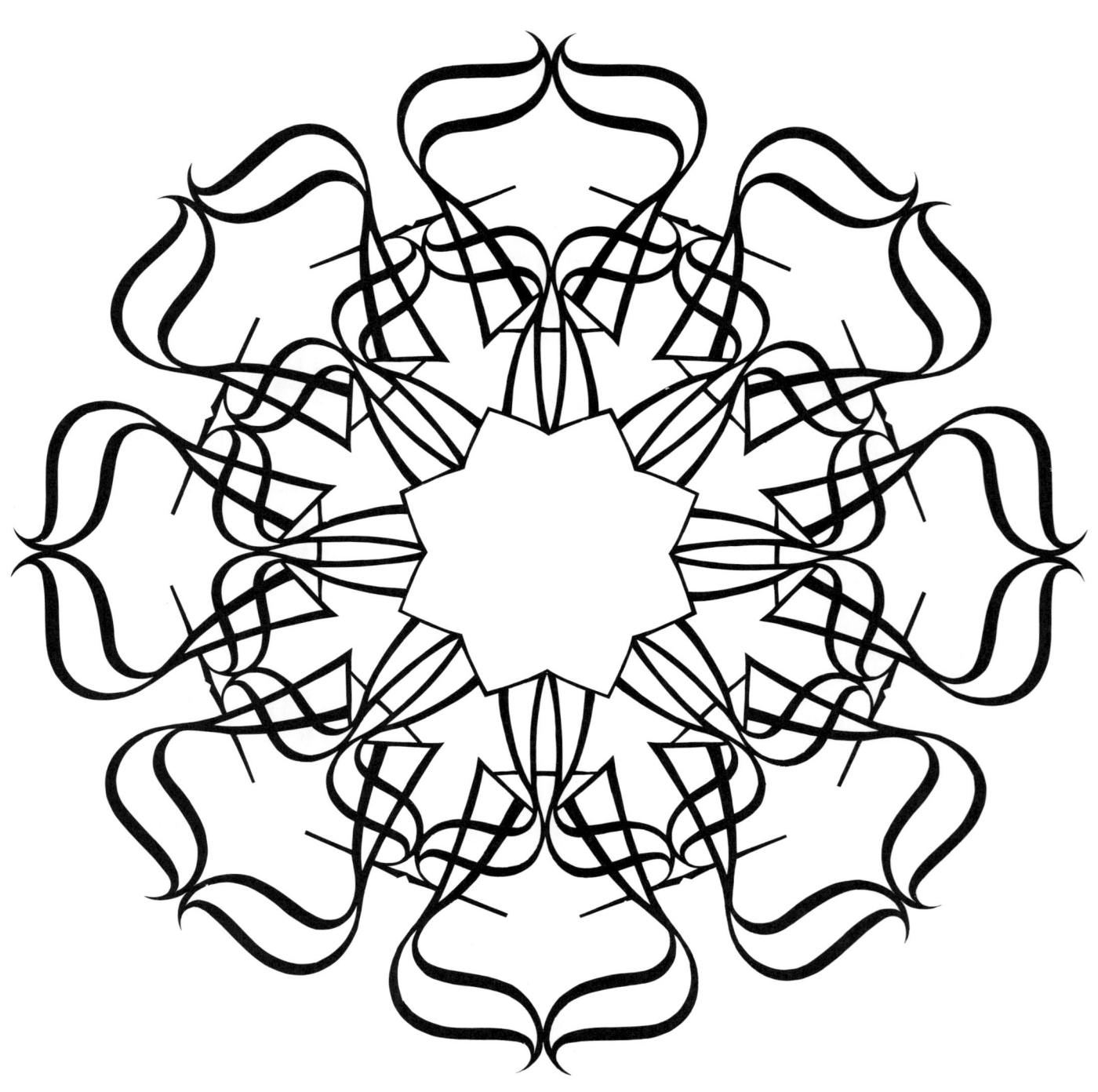